W9-AUS-231

3/01

22.50

Sore Throats *and* Tonsillitis

Dr. Alvin Silverstein,

Virginia Silverstein, and

Laura Silverstein Nunn

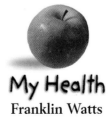

My Health

Franklin Watts

A Division of Grolier Publishing

New York • London • Hong Kong • Sydney

Danbury, Connecticut

Photographs©: Custom Medical Stock Photo: 28 (NMSB), 31 (Saturn Stills/SPL), 33 top (David Weinstein & Associates); Monkmeyer Press: 36 (Randy Matusow), 25 (Siteman); Nance S. Trueworthy: 7, 29, 37; Peter Arnold Inc.: 16 (CDC/LL), 21 (Manfred Kage), 30 (SIU); Photo Researchers: 19, 23 right (Biophoto Associates), 17 (Biophoto Associates/Science Source), 27 (Ken Lax), 6 (Blair Seitz), 26 (Jeanne White); PhotoEdit: 4 (Mary Kate Denny), 12, 18 (Michael Newman); Tony Stone Images: 23 left (Dr. Hans Gelderblom), 32 (S. Lowry/University Ulster), 13 (David Oliver); Visuals Unlimited: 33 bottom (Raymond B. Otero), 10 (SIU).

Cartoons by Rick Stromoski; medical illustrations by Leonard Morgan

Visit Franklin Watts on the Internet at:
http://publishing.grolier.com

Library of Congress Cataloging-in-Publication Data

Silverstein, Alvin.
  Sore throats and tonsillitis / by Alvin Silverstein, Virginia Silverstein, and Laura Silverstein Nunn.
        p.   cm.—(My Health)
  Includes bibliographical references and index.
  Summary: Explains the nature and causes of a sore throat, discusses the immune system, differentiates between strep throat and tonsillitis, and describes how to treat a sore throat.
    ISBN 0-531-11640-9 (lib. bdg.)   0-531-16508-6 (pbk.)
    1. Throat—Disease—Juvenile literature. 2. Tonsillitis—Juvenile literature [1. Throat—Diseases. 2. Tonsillitis. 3. Tonsils.]   I. Silverstein, Virginia B. II. Nunn, Laura Silverstein. III. Title. IV. Series.
RC182.S3 S556   2000
616.3'1—dc21   99-049739

Contents

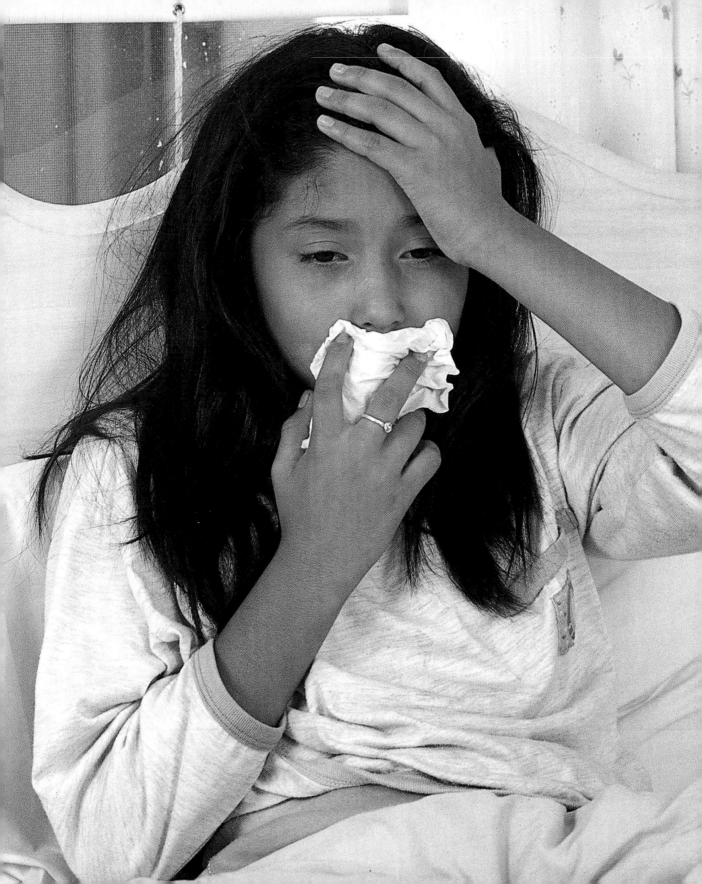

My Throat Hurts

You wake up one morning and your throat feels a little scratchy. At breakfast, you have trouble swallowing your food. Oh no, you have a sore throat! You may even be getting a cold.

A sore throat is often one of the first **symptoms** of a cold. In fact, colds are the most common cause of sore throats. But many other things can make your throat hurt. Your throat may get sore if you yell too much at a football game. Allergies can also make throats sore.

Most sore throats go away in a few days, but sometimes they turn out to be a warning that something dangerous is happening inside your body. So how do you know when your sore throat is serious? Read on to find out.

Did You Know....

Sore throats are one of the most common childhood health complaints.

◀ **A cold can really make you feel miserable.**

What Is the Throat?

Have you ever heard a doctor say, "Stick out your tongue and say 'Ah!'" That doctor wasn't really interested in seeing your tongue. He or she was trying to get a better look at your throat. Your throat can tell a doctor quite a bit about what's going on inside your body.

Stick out your tongue and say "Ah!" The doctor needs to check your throat to see if it is red and swollen.

Shine a flashlight into your mouth and look at your throat in a mirror. The first thing you see is a flap of tissue hanging down in the back. It looks a little bit like a punching bag. That is your *uvula*.

Behind the uvula is the entrance to your throat, or *pharynx*. Your pharynx is a tube that carries air to your lungs, food and water to your stomach, and sounds from your vocal cords to your mouth.

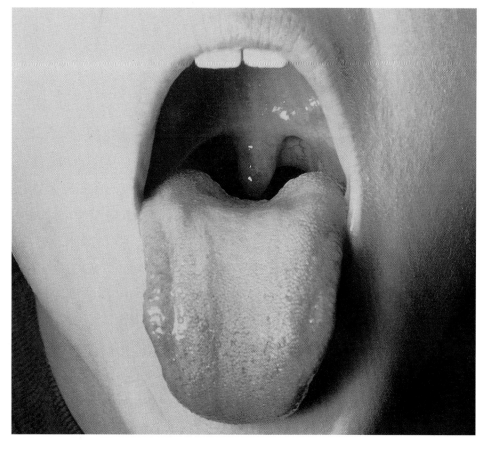

Take a look at the little punching bag—the uvula—at back of this boy's mouth.

Open your mouth and look in a mirror. Can you see your tonsils, uvula, and tongue?

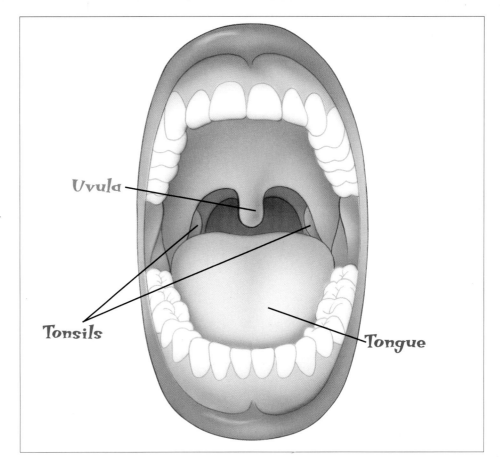

Uvula

Tonsils

Tongue

As you look through the opening to your pharynx, you can see two large rounded blobs of tissue, one at each side. These are your **tonsils**. Healthy tonsils are pink, just like the rest of your throat. Although your tonsils are fairly large, they leave plenty of room for air and food to pass down the tube. When you get a cold or other illnesses, your tonsils may swell up. Sometimes they swell so much that they nearly close off your pharynx.

You can't see it in a mirror, but your pharynx has two branches—the air pipe, or **trachea**, and the food pipe, or **esophagus**. When you swallow, a leaf-shaped trapdoor called the **epiglottis** closes the opening to your trachea. It prevents liquid and food particles from going down your air pipe. Sometimes, usually when you eat too fast, your epiglottis does not close and something "goes down the wrong pipe."

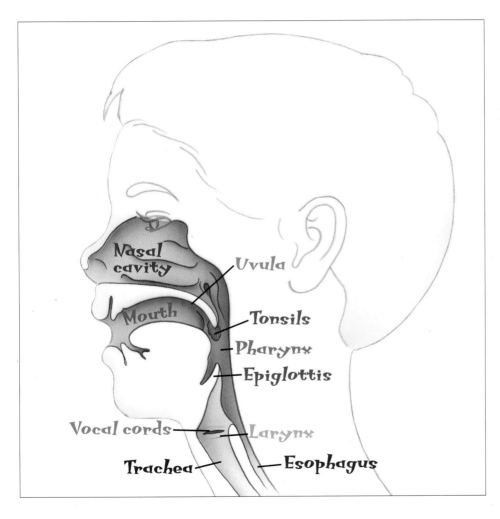

Did you realize that your throat has so many parts?

Look at your neck in the mirror while you swallow. Do you see a lump bulge out and move up and down? That is your voice box, or *larynx*. Your larynx is part of your trachea. There are two folds of tissue stretched out across your larynx. These are your *vocal cords*.

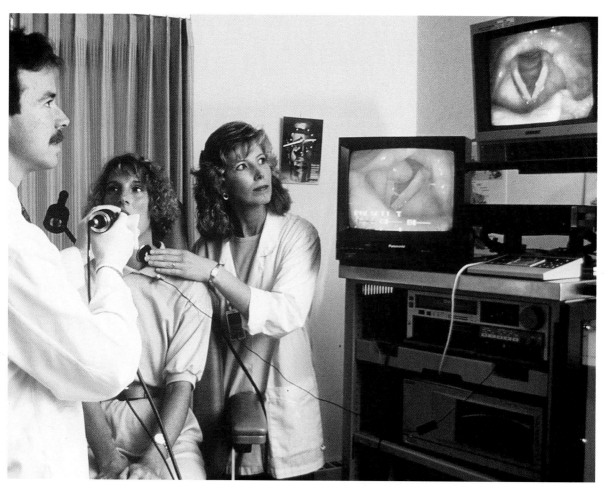

With the help of computer technology, a doctor can examine a patient's vocal cords right in the office.

When your vocal cords are relaxed, there is a wide space between them and air can flow through freely. When you talk or sing, your vocal cords move closer together. As air passes between them, they vibrate and make a sound. The thicker your vocal cords, the lower the sound they make. Women and children have shorter, thinner vocal cords than men. That's why their voices are higher than men's voices.

When You Can't Speak

Have you ever tried to talk, but no sound came out of your throat? That's what happens when you have **laryngitis**. When your larynx gets irritated and your vocal cords swell up, air has trouble moving between your vocal cords. You get laryngitis.

When just a little air can move between your vocal cords, you make sounds that are low, rough, and husky. You have a **hoarse** voice. Laryngitis may be the result of a cold, or it may occur if you yell or cough a lot. Fortunately, laryngitis usually lasts only a few days.

Why Does My Throat Hurt?

A sore throat may be a warning that you are doing something to hurt yourself. If you eat or drink something that is too hot, it may burn the **cells** that line your mouth and throat. Burns can be really painful.

Careful! Don't burn your throat!

Luckily, this kind of burn heals quickly. The damaged cells are soon replaced by healthy new ones. After a day or so, your throat won't hurt any more.

How can yelling give you a sore throat? Touch the inside of your mouth with your fingertip. Does it seem wet? The moisture inside your mouth and throat helps keep the cells that line them soft and flexible.

When you yell or scream, a lot of air moves through your throat. All that air carries away some of the moisture, and the lining starts to dry out. If the lining gets too dry, the cells on top may be damaged. That is why yelling can make your throat sore.

Too much yelling and screaming can really make your throat dry.

Activity 1:
How Does Your Throat Get Dry?

Run the tip of your tongue over the roof of your mouth. It feels moist and slippery. Try pinching your nose closed and breathing with your mouth open for 30 seconds. What does the inside of your mouth feel like now?

Saliva, the watery fluid that constantly flows into your mouth, helps keep the lining moist. How does breathing through your mouth make it dry out?

To find out, wet two sponges and squeeze them out just enough so that they are not dripping. Place one sponge in front of a blowing fan. Place the other sponge away from the flow of air.

After 5 minutes, press a piece of paper towel gently against the surface of each sponge. Are both sponges still wet? If so, test them again after 10, 15, and 20 minutes. How long does it take for the surface of each sponge to dry out? How is this similar to what happened in your mouth?

In winter, the air inside most homes gets dry. Breathing all that dry air can dry your throat and make it a bit sore. Breathing through your mouth, which you may do if your nose is stuffed up by a cold or an allergy, can also make your throat dry and sore.

Sometimes a sore throat is a sign of real trouble. It may mean that your body is being attacked by germs. These germs want to get into your body's cells, where they can get free food and shelter. They don't really mean to cause you harm. They're just looking for a cozy new home.

Beware of Smoke!

People who smoke often get sore throats. When they puff on a cigarette, they breathe in hot, dry smoke and irritating chemicals that can damage their throat cells. Have you ever had a sore throat after being in a room with a person who smokes? That's because some of the cigarette smoke was in the air you breathed.

Have you ever had a cold? Just about everyone has. A cold is caused by a kind of germ called a **virus**. There are more than 200 kinds of cold viruses!

Viruses are so small that you can't see them—not even with an ordinary microscope. Scientists use high-power electron microscopes to look at viruses. How small is a virus? If a virus were the size of an ant, you would be as big as the whole Earth!

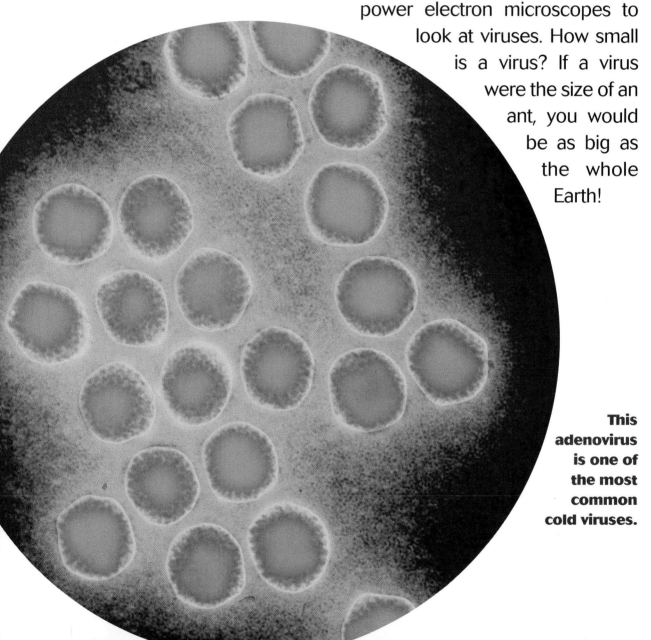

This adenovirus is one of the most common cold viruses.

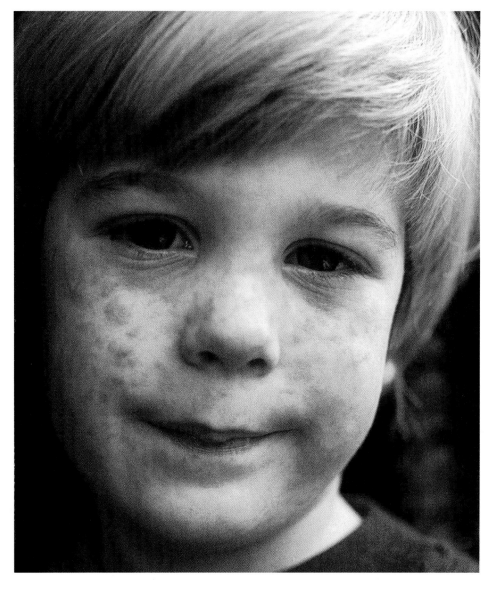

A sore throat may be a sign that you're coming down with measles. The characteristic spots show up a few days later.

A sore throat can also be the first symptom of chickenpox or measles. These illnesses are caused by viruses too.

Stay Away from Aspirin

DIRECTIONS: Adults, take 1 or 2 tablets with water every 4 hours, as needed, up to a maximum of 12 tablets per 24 hours. WARNINGS: Children and teenagers should not use this medicine for chicken pox or flu symptoms before a doctor is consulted about Reye syndrome, a rare but serious illness reported to be associated with aspirin. Do not take if: allergic to aspirin; have asthma; for pain for more than 10 days or for fever for more than 3 days unless directed by a doctor. If pain or fever persists or gets worse, if new symptoms occur, or if redness or swelling is present, consult a doctor because these could be signs of a serious condition. Keep out of reach of children. In case of accidental overdose, contact a doctor immediately. As with any drug, if you are pregnant or nursing a baby, seek the advice of a health professional before using this product. IT IS ESPECIALLY IMPORTANT NOT TO USE ASPIRIN DURING THE LAST 3 MONTHS OF PREGNANCY UNLESS SPECIFICALLY DIRECTED TO DO SO BY A DOCTOR BECAUSE IT MAY CAUSE PROBLEMS IN THE UNBORN CHILD OR COMPLICATIONS DURING DELIVERY. Do not take if you have stomach problems (such as heartburn, upset stomach or stomach pain) that persist or recur, or if you have ulcers or bleeding problems, unless directed by a doctor. If ringing in the ears or loss of hearing occurs, consult a doctor before taking again. Consult a dentist promptly for toothache. DRUG INTERACTION PRECAUTION: Do not take this product if you are taking a prescription drug for anticoagulation (thinning of the blood), diabetes, gout or arthritis unless directed by a doctor. ACTIVE INGREDIENT: 325 mg Aspirin per tablet. INACTIVE INGREDIENTS: Carnauba Wax, Glyceryl Triacetate, Hydroxypropyl Methylcellulose, Starch, Talc. May also contain: Dicaicium Phosphate Dihydrate, Microcrystalline Cellulose, Silicon Dioxide, Stearic Acid.
Avoid excessive heat (over 104°F or 40°C).
*Good Neighbor Pharmacy Aspirin is not manufactured or distributed by The Bayer Company, Sterling Health, Division of Sterling Winthrop, Inc., distributor of Bayer®.

DISTRIBUTED BY
Bergen Brunswig
Drug Company
ORANGE CA
92613-9810

EXP09/00
87JC195
L 416 85 29 BA

0 87701 94842
BBC# 948-422

Adults often take aspirin to help relieve cold symptoms, but kids should stay away from aspirin. A child who takes aspirin may develop **Reye's syndrome**, a disease that affects the liver and nervous system. Children should take acetaminophen (uh-SEE-tuh-MIN-uh-fuhn) instead of aspirin.

Children should stay away from aspirin. If you look at the label on an aspirin bottle, you'll see a warning that young people who take aspirin may develop Reye's syndrome.

Another kind of germ, called a **bacterium**, can also cause illnesses that may give you a sore throat. Bacteria are much larger than viruses, but they are still too small to see without a microscope.

Bacteria are always growing on your skin and inside your body. To see what bacteria look like, scrape off some of the material around the bottom of your teeth and look at it under a microscope. The bacteria will look like little balls or sticks.

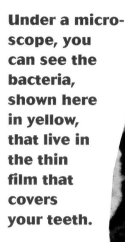

Under a micro-scope, you can see the bacteria, shown here in yellow, that live in the thin film that covers your teeth.

Most of the bacteria that live on or inside your body are harmless. For example, the bacteria in your intestines break down food so that you can **digest** it more easily. Some kinds of bacteria can make you sick. One kind of bacterium makes an acid that eats away at your teeth and causes cavities. Another kind of bacterium causes strep throat.

The Body's Defenses

When bacteria and viruses get inside you, your body fights back. Some of the germs that enter your nose get trapped in bristly hairs inside your nostrils. Germs that sneak past these hairs fall into a gooey fluid that covers the lining of your nose. This fluid is called **mucus**. Mucus carries the trapped germs to the back of your throat. When you swallow, these germs—plus germs that have entered your mouth—travel to your stomach where they are destroyed in a pool of acid.

Other invading germs are destroyed by cells in your **immune system**. When viruses and bacteria get inside your cells, those cells call for help. They do this by sending out chemicals that alert your immune system to the danger. It doesn't take long for an army of **white blood cells** to arrive. Like good soldiers, these cells identify invading germs and destroy them.

Some of the white blood cells make special chemicals called **antibodies**. They fit into the virus, just as a key fits into a lock. Antibodies may kill germs, or they may make it easier for your white blood cells to destroy them.

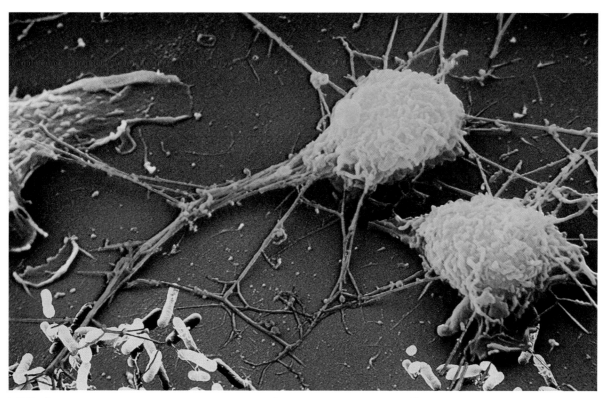

This image was taken through a microscope. Two white blood cells (blue) are attacking a group of bacteria (yellow).

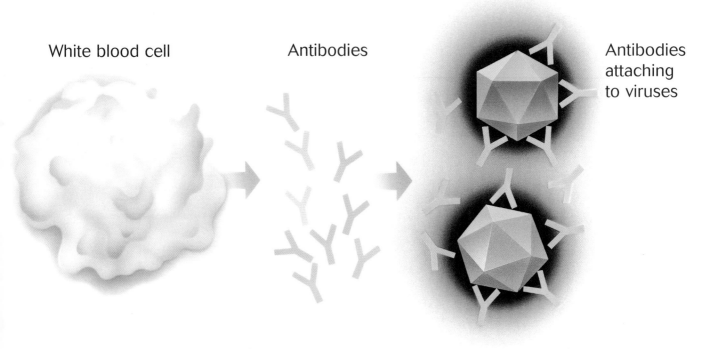

White blood cell

Antibodies

Antibodies attaching to viruses

When viruses invade your body, some white blood cells produce antibodies. The antibodies attach to the viruses and help destroy them.

Once the body has made antibodies against a specific disease germ, it keeps some copies even when the illness is over. Then, if the same kind of germ invades your body again, the antibodies can quickly make a whole new army of antibodies to fight the invaders.

That's why you can only get chickenpox or measles once in your life. If the germs that cause these diseases enter your body a second time, your antibodies destroy them right away—before they get a chance to make you sick.

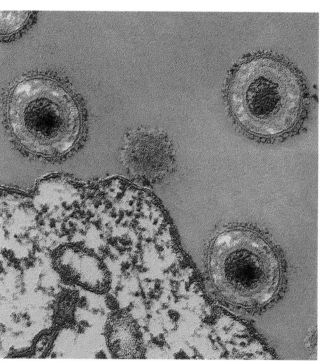

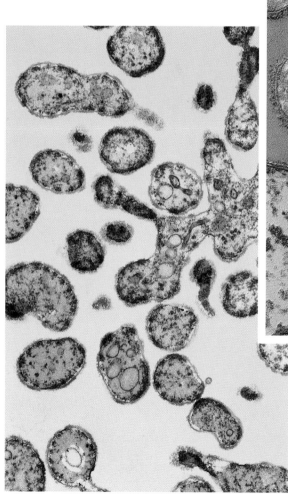

These images were taken through a microscope. They show three chickenpox viruses getting ready to attack a cell (above), and measles viruses that have multiplied inside an infected cell and are now being released to attack other body cells (left).

Catching a Cold

Kids catch more colds than adults. Every time you have a cold, your immune system makes antibodies to fight the virus that causes it and saves some of them. That means you are protected. You won't get a cold caused by the same virus again. Parents and teachers catch more colds than most other adults because they're around children so much.

Colds are a different story. There are so many different kinds of cold viruses that when you catch a cold, chances are that it is not the same virus that made you sick last year or the year before. That's why most people catch between 50 and 200 colds in their lifetime.

Your immune system works hard to protect you against invading disease germs, but it also causes some of the things that make you feel so miserable. Sometimes the chemicals that damaged cells use to call for help tell the brain to raise your body temperature. This is why you get a **fever**.

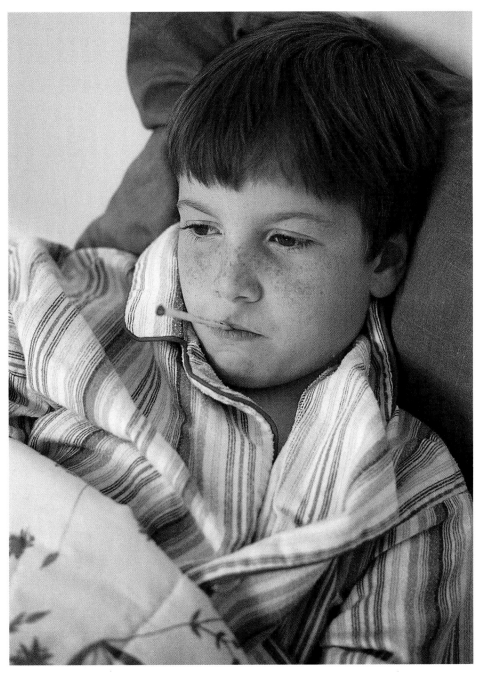

Have you ever had a fever? When your body temperature rises, it means your immune system is working hard to fight disease germs.

What Is an Allergy?

Sometimes the immune system is a little too active. It thinks that something harmless, such as food or dog hair, is a threat. This is what happens in people who have an **allergy**. A sore throat may be the result of an allergic reaction. About 50 million people in the United States have allergies. That means one out of every five people is allergic to something.

If you are allergic to dog hair, you may get a sore throat from all that sneezing and coughing.

The same chemicals cause the walls of the tiny blood vessels in your skin to get leaky. Fluid seeps out of the cells and the whole area becomes red and swollen. When the lining of your nose swells, you have trouble breathing. Some of the fluid dribbles out, giving you a runny nose.

If particles of fluid get caught on the hairs in your nose, your brain sends a message to your chest muscles, and you sneeze. Some of the fluid drips down the back of your swollen throat and irritates it. The result is a sore throat.

This girl is wiping her runny nose with a tissue.

What Is Tonsillitis?

For years, people believed that tonsils were useless blobs of tissue. They often became red and swollen when a person was sick, and seemed like easy targets for infections. If a child had **tonsillitis**—inflammation of the tonsils—several times, doctors usually took out the child's tonsils.

These swollen tonsils may look gross and painful, but they contain helpful disease-fighting cells that attack invading germs.

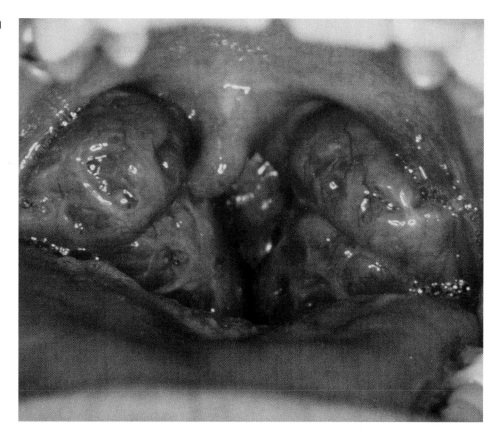

Things are quite different today. Doctors now know that your tonsils are a very important part of your immune system. These blobs of tissue are filled with special disease-fighting cells that trap invading germs and destroy them before they get a chance to reach the lungs. Many doctors believe that when the tonsils get red and swollen, they are just doing their job. They are busy fighting germs.

Nevertheless, children who get tonsillitis three or four times a year may need to have their tonsils taken out—especially if the tonsils swell up so much that it is difficult to eat and drink. When this happens, the tonsils are no longer helping the body. A **tonsillectomy** is a routine operation today. The patient can usually go home the same day. After the operation, the patient's throat will be sore and he or she will not be able to swallow solid foods for a while. Soft foods, such as ice cream, Jello, and pudding, are good choices after a tonsillectomy.

After a tonsillectomy, a spoonful of ice cream will sooth your sore throat.

When tonsils are infected, they swell and ooze pus.

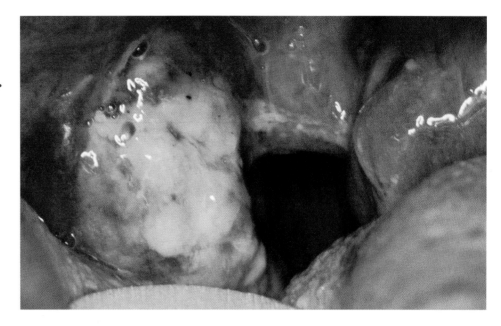

How do you know whether you have tonsillitis? If you do, your tonsils will look red and swollen and may have patches of white or yellowish **pus**. Your throat will be very sore, and you will have a hard time swallowing—especially when you eat or drink. You may also have a high fever, a headache, or an earache. If you have any of these problems for more than 2 to 3 days, you should see a doctor. When properly treated, tonsillitis goes away in a few days.

Tonsillitis can be caused by both viruses and bacteria, but most cases are caused by bacterial infections. A kind of medicine called an **antibiotic** can be used to treat bacterial infections, but not viral infections.

What Is Strep Throat?

If you have a sore throat, a high fever, and white or yellow patches on your tonsils or the back of your throat, you may have an infection called **strep throat**. Other symptoms of strep throat may include swollen tonsils, a headache, a stomachache, and swollen **lymph nodes** in the neck.

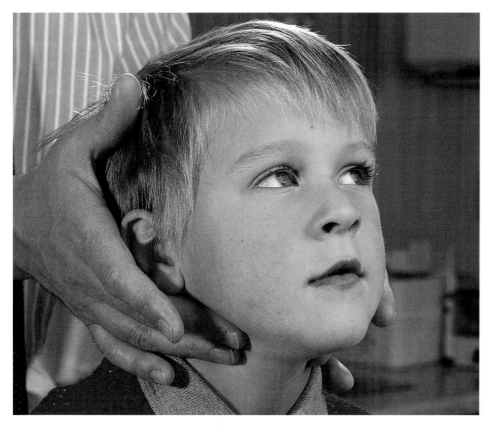

A doctor is checking this boy's lymph nodes to see if they are swollen. If they are, he may have strep throat or some other illness.

Strep throat is caused by *Streptococcus* bacteria. About 10 percent of all sore throats are caused by these bacteria, and between 20 and 30 percent of all throat infections are the result of strep. Strep infections often lead to tonsillitis.

Strep throat is not easy to diagnose just by looking at a person's throat. The best way to diagnose this infection is with a **throat culture**.

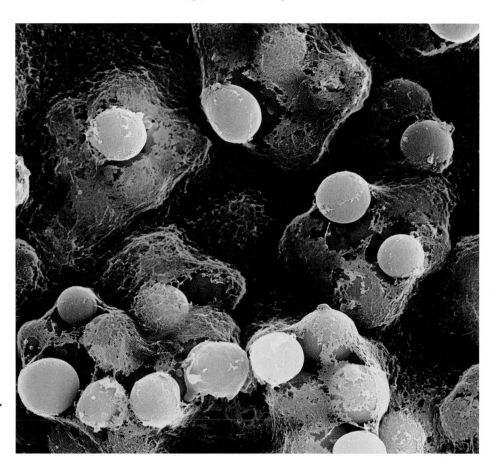

These *Streptococcus pyogenes* bacteria can give you a painful sore throat. (Pyogenes means "pus-forming"—a good name for strep throat bacteria!)

How a Throat Culture Works

To do a throat culture, a doctor or nurse wipes the back of your throat with a cotton swab. The swab picks up saliva and some of the bacteria on the lining of your throat.

The swab is wiped onto the surface of a flat plastic dish that is filled with a jelly-like material. The dish is then placed in an incubator—a box that is kept at the same temperature as your body. Under these conditions, the bacteria grow quickly and reproduce by splitting in half. The number of bacteria in the dish can double in just 20 minutes!

After a day or so, there are so many bacteria that they can be seen as a spot on the surface of the jelly. Because the spots formed by different kinds of bacteria have different colors, shapes, and textures, scientists can often tell whether there were any strep bacteria in your throat by looking at the spots. Just to be safe, though, they also look at the bacteria under a microscope.

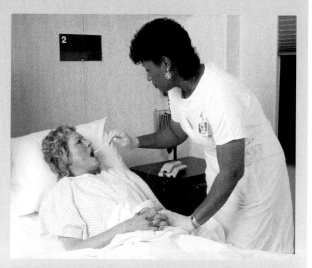

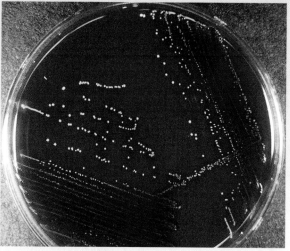

A throat culture test can show whether a strep infection is present (top). After a few days in a petri dish, the *Streptococcus* bacteria have multiplied greatly (bottom).

Who Gets Strep?

Strep throat is most common in children between 5 and 12 years old. In the United States, up to 20 million children develop strep infections each year. Sometimes the infection is so serious that the child must be treated in a hospital.

If your throat culture shows that you have strep throat, your doctor will want you to start taking an antibiotic right away. Most of the time, you will be able to go back to school the next day.

It is important to take all the antibiotic medicine that the doctor gives you. Don't stop taking it just because you start to feel better. When you do not take all of the medicine the doctor gave you, some of the bacteria may survive and multiply. If these new **drug-resistant germs** are passed on to other people, they will not be helped by the same antibiotic that made you feel better. After a while, the antibiotic may become useless in fighting strep infections.

When you have strep throat, your immune system makes antibodies to fight *Streptococcus* bacteria.

Some of the chemicals on *Streptococcus* bacteria are similar to chemicals found in your joints and heart. If strep throat is not treated, your antibodies may accidentally attack the cells in your **joints** and heart. This causes a disease called **rheumatic fever**.

At one time, many children developed rheumatic fever. Now that we have antibiotics to treat strep infections, rheumatic fever is much less common.

Strep and More Strep

You can get strep throat many times in your life. More than 120 different varieties of *Streptococcus* bacteria can cause the disease. Scientists have recently developed a **vaccine** that can stop all the bacteria that cause strep throat. When a doctor sprays the vaccine into your nose, you will be immune to strep throat.

SPLORT!

How Can I Soothe My Sore Throat?

Sore throats can be very painful, but there are several things you can do to make your throat feel better.

- Try to keep your throat moist. Run a **humidifier** in your home during the winter. When you fill a humidifier with water and turn it on, it changes the water into water vapor and pumps it into the air.

A humidifier helps to keep a sore throat moist.

- Hard candy and throat lozenges can also soothe sore throats. They get the saliva flowing in your mouth and help keep your throat moist.

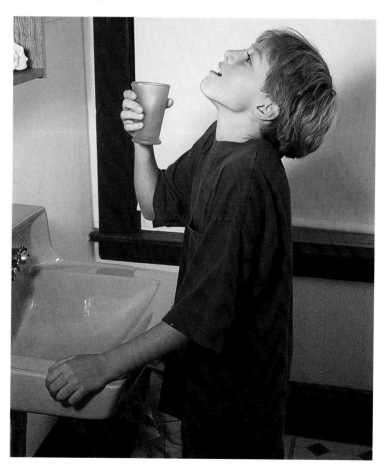

- Drinking plenty of fluids keeps sore throats from getting dry. Hot tea with honey can also have a soothing effect. Some medical experts recommend gargling warm salt water to help sore throats. (Add 1/2 teaspoon of salt to 1 cup of warm water.)

- Acetaminophen, an aspirin substitute that does not cause Reye's syndrome, will also help to relieve the pain of a sore throat.

- Rest your voice. The more you talk, the drier your throat will become, and the more it will hurt.

Gargling a salt water solution can soothe a sore throat.

Activity 2:
Why Does a Dry Throat Hurt?

Start with two old, dry kitchen sponges. Try to bend one in half. Does it bend easily, or does it crack? Wet the other sponge, squeeze out the excess water, and try bending it in half. What happens?

The cells lining your mouth and throat are similar to a sponge. They need to be moist to stay flexible. If they dry out, they may crack when you swallow or talk.

Of course, the best way to help your throat is to avoid getting sore throats in the first place. You can cut down on the number of sore throats you get by staying away from people with colds or strep throat and not handling any objects they have touched. You should also do everything you can to keep yourself healthy. Eat healthy foods, get plenty of sleep, and exercise every day. Wash your hands and body regularly, wear clean clothes, use clean dishes, and wash your food before you eat it. If your immune system stays strong, it will be able to fight off nasty germs.

Glossary

allergy—an overreaction of the immune system to a normally harmless substance, resulting in a sore throat, a rash, sneezing, breathing difficulties, or other symptoms

antibiotic—a drug that kills bacteria

antibody—a protein produced by white blood cells; some antibodies help to kill germs

bacterium (plural **bacteria**)—a tiny living thing that is too small to see without a microscope; some bacteria cause diseases

cell—the basic unit of all living things

digest—to break down food so that it can be used by the body

drug-resistant germ—a bacterium or virus that is not killed by an antibiotic

epiglottis—a leaf-shaped structure that closes off the trachea when liquids or solids are being swallowed

esophagus—the food pipe; a tube that leads from the throat to the stomach

fever—a body temperature that is higher than normal

hoarse—a voice that is low and harsh sounding

humidifier—an electrical device that changes liquid water into water vapor and sprays the vapor into the air

immune system—the body's disease-fighting system; includes white blood cells, the lymph nodes, and the tonsils

joint—a place where two bones meet

laryngitis—a swelling of the throat caused by an infection. It often causes hoarseness.

larynx—the voice box; the part of the trachea that contains the vocal cords and produces sounds when air passes through it

lymph node—one of the small structures in the body that contain disease-fighting cells

mucus—a slimy fluid that coats the inside of the mouth, nose, and throat

pharynx—the throat; the passage that leads from the mouth and nose to the trachea (air pipe) and esophagus (food pipe)

pus—whitish or yellowish liquid in infected tissues. Pus is made up of dead white blood cells and germs.

Reye's syndrome—an illness that damages the liver and respiratory system. It may develop when young people with a viral infection take aspirin.

rheumatic fever—an illness that may follow a strep infection; the immune system mistakenly attacks the body's own tissues and may damage the joints, heart, or kidneys

saliva—the watery fluid in the mouth that keeps the tissues moist

strep throat—an infection of the throat lining by *Streptococcus* bacteria; if untreated, it may develop into rheumatic fever

symptom—an indication of illness

throat culture—a test for strep throat

tonsillectomy—surgery to remove the tonsils

tonsillitis—inflammation of the tonsils

tonsils—two large blobs of tissue in the throat just behind of the mouth cavity

trachea—the air pipe; a tube with muscular walls that leads from the throat to the lungs

uvula—a flap of tissue that hangs down from the roof of the mouth at the entrance to the throat

vaccine—a substance that stimulates the body's disease-fighting cells to produce antibodies against a particular kind of germ

virus—a tiny germ that may cause disease. It can survive only inside living cells.

vocal cords—two small folds of tissue that stretch across the larynx

white blood cell—a cell that fights invading germs and other foreign substances

Learning More

Books

Burles, Kenneth T. *Tonsillitis*. Vero Beach, FL: Rourke Press, 1998.

Demuth, Patricia Brennan. *Achoo!: All About Colds*. New York: Grosset & Dunlap, 1997.

Silverstein, Dr. Alvin, Virginia Silverstein, and Laura Silverstein Nunn. *Allergies*. Danbury, CT: Franklin Watts, 1999.

Silverstein, Dr. Alvin, Virginia Silverstein, and Laura Silverstein Nunn. *Common Colds*. Danbury, CT: Franklin Watts, 1999.

Stille, Darlene R. *The Respiratory System*. Danbury, CT: Children's Press, 1997.

Winn, Marie. *The Sick Book*. New York: Four Winds Press, 1976.

Organizations and Online Sites

American Academy of Family Physicians
8880 Ward Parkway
Kansas City, MO 64114-2797

American Academy of Otolaryngology-Head and Neck Surgery
One Prince Street
Alexandria, VA 22314-3357

Hoarseness Prevention & Treatment Tips
http://www.netdoor.com/entinfo/hoarsaao.html
If you have laryngitis, you may find some helpful advice at this site.

Mommy, I Have a Sore Throat
http://www.mayohealth.org/mayo/9510/htm/strep.htm
This site is maintained by the Mayo Clinic.

Rheumatic Fever
http://www.luhs.org/health/infe/infe4726.htm
This site features information from the Loyola University Health System.

Self-Care: Tonsillitis
http://www.mcare.org/healthtips/homecare/tonsilli.htm
This site will provide you with background information about tonsillitis as well as advice for treating the illness.

Sore Throat
http://www.healthy.net/library/books/smart/SoreThroat.htm
This site is one section from the book *Smart Medicine for a Healthier Child* by Janet Zand.

A Sore Throat

http://www.aomc.org/sorethroat.html

If you are looking for information about sore throats or want to know whether you should see a doctor, check out this site.

Sore Throats: Causes and Cures

http://www.netdoor.com/entinfo/throaaao.html

The information at this site comes from the American Academy of Otolaryngology-Head and Neck Surgery.

For Sore Throats

http://www3.pitt.edu/~cjm6/scthroat.html

This site features practical suggestions for soothing a sore throat.

Strep Throat

http://www.columbia.net/schools/element/strepn.html

This site has all kinds of information about strep throat.

Tonsillitis: What Is It? When Is Surgery Necessary?

http://www.brianmachidamd.com/tonsillitis.htm

Get answers to all your questions about tonsillitis and tonsil-lectomy.

When You Have a Sore Throat

http://www.aafp.org/patientinfo/sorethro.html

This site features facts and advice from the American Academy of Family Physicians

Index

About the Authors

Dr. Alvin Silverstein is a Professor of Biology at the College of Staten Island of the City University of New York. **Virginia Silverstein** is a translator of Russian scientific literature. The Silversteins first worked together on a research project at the University of Pennsylvania. Since then, they have produced 6 children and more than 150 published books for young people.

Laura Silverstein Nunn, a graduate of Kean College, has been helping with her parents' books since her high school days. She is the coauthor of more than twenty books on diseases and health, science concepts, endangered species, and pets. Laura lives with her husband Matt and their young son Cory in a rural New Jersey town not far from her childhood home.